I THOUGHT SO—

A Book of Epigrams

~:~

Michael Lipsey

LOST
COAST
PRESS

I Thought So–
A Book of Epigrams

Copyright ©2008 by Michael Lipsey

Lost Coast Press
155 Cypress Street
Fort Bragg, CA 95437
(800) 773-7782
www.cypresshouse.com

Cover and book design: Michael Brechner / Cypress House
Cover illustration: © iStockphoto.com/Janne Ahvo

LIBRARY OF CONGRESS CATALOGING-IN-PUBLICATION DATA

Lipsey, Michael, 1941-
  I thought so : a book of epigrams / Michael Lipsey. -- 1st ed.
  p. cm.
  ISBN-13: 978-1-882897-94-0 (pbk. : alk. paper)
  1. Epigrams. I. Title.
  PS3612.I67I25 2008
  811'.6--dc22   2007030526

PRINTED IN THE USA
2 4 6 8 9 7 5 3 1

～∷～

Shut not your doors to me proud libraries,
For that which was lacking on all your well-fill'd shelves,
yet needed most, I bring,
… a book I have made,
The words of my book nothing, the drift of it everything.

Walt Whitman, Book I, *Leaves of Grass*

～∷～

For Louise,
who brightens my life.
And to my parents, who always
encouraged my many interests.

Contents

I THOUGHT SO—

~:~

Dost thou think I care for a satire or an epigram?
— Shakespeare

The epigrammarian, or epigrammist, practices an old and poorly paid profession. An introduction to a book of epigrams is bound to seem tedious. Would that I could condense it into one line: An epigram is a few words equaling many, a distilled thought. *Webster's Dictionary* defines an epigram as "A concise, clever, often paradoxical statement."

In the ancient world, the first epigrams were inscriptions in verse, carved into the stones of tombs, statues, temples, and triumphal arches. Later, with the convenience of paper, they evolved into short pieces of wisdom, often witty or satiric.

What is the difference between an epigram or a maxim, and a proverb, saying, aphorism, or adage? There is no clear boundary. They are all short, pithy, and to the point. But proverbs and sayings are usually simple folk wisdom; they can be truisms and or even nonsensical. An epigram or a maxim is usually more elegant and often has an ironic twist.

"Proverbial wisdom" is everyday, common wisdom. "A penny saved is a penny earned" is a mere proverb, essentially the literal words of Ben Franklin. But suppose you saved a penny you found on the sidewalk—would you have earned it? "A stitch in time saves nine." Could be—or maybe it's time to throw away those baggy-kneed pants.

"Nothing prevents us from being natural so much as the desire to appear so." La Rochefoucauld sets us thinking about situations in which we have tried to appear at ease and failed. This maxim has been in print for around 350 years. The Duke de la Rochefoucauld is the gold standard in maxims, but he tends to be morose, having lost a few lovers, battles, and castles. Here is a selection of his maxims:

> *"No people are more often wrong than those who cannot bear to be."*

> *"There are ways of curing madness, but none of righting the wrong-headed."*

> *"It is more important to study men than books."*

> *"We enjoy seeing through others, but not being seen through."*

> *"It is not possible to enumerate all the kinds of vanity."*

An epigram can convey a large idea, such as Samuel Johnson's

> *"Marriage has many pains, but celibacy has no pleasures."*

Nine words that summarize the RELATIONSHIP and SEXUALITY sections at your local bookstore.

A good epigram makes you think, *Well, that's so true, and I've never thought of it in that way.*

> *Men argue, nature acts.*
> — Voltaire

I've always enjoyed reading books of quotations, sayings, and proverbs. After years of browsing them I began my modest career as an epigrammist, which requires not modesty, but plenty of *chutzpah* (Yiddish: an excess of confidence unjustified by one's circumstances). Who am I, a nobody, to say something immortal? Well, there are no degrees or prerequisites for writing epigrams. Epictetus was a slave, La Rochefoucauld a duke, Kafka a government bureaucrat, William Blake a starving artist, and Nietzsche was a nut case.

We get pleasure in reading maxims, but the quotable is also useful to us—in writing a speech, making a toast at a wedding, to begin an article, in a sermon, to inscribe in a book given as a gift, in making a point in an argument, in an obituary, before a poem, in concluding a novel ("All is vanity"). Why struggle with a thought if someone has already said it better? And of course I am sending my epigrams out into the world in the hope that they will be usefully quoted.

I have made every effort to avoid restating epigrams I've read elsewhere. But it is possible, in fact likely, that something in this book has appeared elsewhere, either by pure coincidence or because I once read it but have the delusion that it was my original thought. If so, I apologize and will remove from future editions anything not original that should be called to my attention.

The epigrams in this book are sectioned into the traditional categories and I have attempted to present them in a meaningful array. We begin with MANNERS because one is nothing without them. I have included an ATTITUDE section only because I am a creature of my times. In these times one attempts to be a Positive Person and to avoid Negativity. The best way to do this is to get a lobotomy. I admit that my ATTITUDE section is somewhat contradicted by all the other sections, but consistency is the hobgoblin of little minds, such as those who warn against beginning sentences with adverbs.

One does not read a book of epigrams like a novel; one properly skips around in it. But then, one often skips around in any kind of book, except a mystery. Most readers will start with HEALTH, then LOVE and WEALTH. FOOD and TRAVEL will get some attention. Some will foolishly flip past the valuable lessons contained in MANNERS, MORALITY, and VANITY. I will forgive those who choose to skip DEATH.

And now a word about me. My favorite author's note is by Edward Lear:

How pleasant to know Mr. Lear!
Who has written such volumes of stuff!
Some think him ill-tempered and queer,
But a few think him pleasant enough.

I would like to believe that people find me pleasant enough. Happily married, I find myself, to my surprise, a senior suburbanite, retired and fussing over a garden regularly plundered by fearless suburban deer. Mornings are reserved for coffee and grumbling over the papers. A passionate cook, I am master of our kitchen, if nothing else. In the evenings, I put on long pants and we go out in search of the music and dance that we love.

I am somewhat religious, but God and I have come to an understanding that I am allowed to form my own opinions about the supernatural, divine law, theology, and organized religion. I require music to feel the presence of the divine. My political opinions range from left to right, depending on the issue at hand and who is at hand to discuss that issue. A follower of any ideology is a person who has not learned to think for herself. If I am a follower of anything, that thing is classic Stoic philosophy. If you would like to know what that is, read Zeno of Citium, Epictetus, Marcus Aurelius, or more conveniently, this book.

Do not let yourself be deluded by anyone; this is all I teach.

— Rinzai

People everywhere are interesting, if you are interested in people. I like people who are very open about their lives. I like straight talk. I don't enjoy being with people who try to seem like something more than they are, smarter or more successful. But I especially delight in people who are informed and who have their own opinions about things. Or people who are doing interesting things, right now. Original ideas and original visions are what make life interesting for the rest of us.

> *Imagination is more important than knowledge.*
> — Albert Einstein

I was born with a severely diminished ability to respect authority, which has not improved with age. My wardrobe may have improved, but I still think the 1960s were the best time in history to be young, and even better, to be in California. Obviously, a person such as myself was fairly unemployable and so I had to make my way in the world disguised as the owner of a small business. Despite the annoyance of having had to make a living, I have always devoted my serious attention to creative endeavors of one sort or another. For me, there is nothing but art.

> *An inveterate and incurable itch for writing besets many.*
> — Juvenal, about AD 128

1 ———————————————————————

It is easy to forgive an insult,
but harder to forget one.

∾∶∾

Gossip slithers into my ear; may it die there.

∾∶∾

Don't worry what people think about you,
because they rarely do.

∾∶∾

Have sympathy for any personality
defect, except cynicism.

∾∶∾

We sink financially in order to rise socially.

∾∶∾

Difficult people are like potholes: there is nothing
to do but go around them.

∾∶∾

The cell phone has exhausted all conversational
possibilities, and still people are chattering
everywhere, about nothing.

~:~

Hide your intensity, or it will scare people.

~:~

An angry face is never a pretty face.

~:~

Some people tend their grudges
as others tend their gardens.

~:~

When we socialize we observe, gossip, schmooze,
and keep score, and on the way home we compare
notes with our partner in our researches.

~:~

We do not like to believe that
we deserve to be anyone's enemy.

~:~

People who always speak their minds
have their fans, but they are few.

∼:∼

Other people are often quite boring,
but we are never boring.

∼:∼

Good character expands your circle of
acquaintance and poor character shrinks it.

∼:∼

Some people are always at a simmer,
ready to boil over.

∼:∼

The wine you serve your guests is of no
consequence compared to the topic you serve.

∼:∼

If you are a fast talker you want to
pick up a slow talker and shake him.

∼:∼

The best method of dealing with
difficult people is the distance method.

~:~

We feel slighted when not invited,
even to a very boring social event.

~:~

Your travels, your possessions, and your health…
is this the drab inventory of your conversation?

~:~

Even a softly spoken insinuation
does not escape our hearing.

~:~

One must endure a monologue,
but one does not have to listen to it.

~:~

A complainer complains as
naturally as a bird sings.

~:~

The last people to arrive are the ones
who always seem to be in a hurry.

~:~

If people said what was actually on their minds
twice as often, the murder rate would double.

~:~

Bad table manners ruin more
careers than incompetence.

~:~

A good listener has no idea
what you are about to say.

~:~

There is nothing ruder than to be a guest
who is obviously not having a good time.

~:~

There is no such thing as an impatient listener,
because there is no listening without patience.

~:~

Easy to say far more than you intended to
when you are being amusing.

∼:∼

Ever heard of anyone being
admired for being a gossip?

∼:∼

A difficult person does not have an easy life.

∼:∼

Don't try to build bridges
with people who burn them.

∼:∼

Speech increases in flavor
as you descend in society.

∼:∼

You would be less rude to telemarketers if you
considered how unfortunate it is to be one.

∼:∼

The juicier the gossip the more
it diminishes the teller.

~:~

Why do kindly people usually look that way?

~:~

Never begin your thanks with
"You shouldn't have…."

~:~

Angry people are most alive when in a rage.

~:~

We have an absolute right to mind our own business.

~:~

To simply be a nice person
is no small achievement.

~:~

I see a crying infant in the face of the angry man.

~:~

One doesn't just become an old bore,
one must serve one's time as a young bore.

~:~

Some people would rather lose the
relationship than the argument.

~:~

The essence of manners is tact,
which few can master.

~:~

"I always tell it like it is" is the long way
of saying, "I'm a jerk."

~:~

Remember only your own stupidity.

~:~

Sarcasm and cynicism are easy,
but irony is mastered by few.

~:~

A party to fulfill social obligations
is not a party, it is a ceremony.

~:~

To appear confident is almost as good
as actually being confident.

~:~

Don't make a pretense of
modesty by denigrating praise.

~:~

A proper elevator expression is
friendly but neutral.

~:~

You never really get to know a taciturn person.

~:~

A braying laugh betrays humble origins, despite
layers of refinement laid on like frosting.

~:~

It is a rare privilege to encounter
greatness—unless the great one happens to be in a
foul mood, jet-lagged, or half-drunk.

~:~

If you could meet your great-great-great grandfather,
you probably would find him very smelly.

~:~

If you don't want to raise bigots,
consider what comes out of your mouth.

~:~

An apology that is followed with a justification is
no apology at all.

~:~

Never tell anyone who is proudly displaying a new
possession that you know where they
could have gotten it for less.

~:~

Good manners can be taught, but not the warmth
of spirit that gives them meaning.

~:~

2

See everything for the first time.

∼:∼

Sing the blues, if you must, but don't live them.

∼:∼

"I'm having a bad day" is a self-fulfilling prophecy.

∼:∼

The biggest head start is a good attitude.

∼:∼

If you fail to understand failure—you can walk
through fire.

∼:∼

On a day like this I feel like I could… but every
day is a day like this!

∼:∼

The pains in your legs are a pleasure, when you're nearing the top.

~:~

Don't waste good news on a pessimist.

~:~

On the morning of the last day of Pompeii the people had many important things on their minds.

~:~

The reason the water is so cold is that you are only in it up to your knees.

~:~

Optimists and pessimists resemble each other in that they are both vertebrates.

~:~

Could you give me a hand? I'm moving the world.

~:~

You can always give yourself one more chance.

~:~

When you toss a cat in the air it always lands on
its feet—there are people like that.

~:~

Never say bad things about anyone
and you will be adored.

~:~

Be a warm person.

~:~

To an awakened mind the best place is here and
the best time is now.

~:~

Welcome yourself to the day with a smile in the
bathroom mirror.

~:~

If you really believe that all men are created equal,
you are comfortable in any company.

~:~

Always keep your charm turned on.

~:~

Be kind to yourself.

~:~

The best advice ever given is "Let it go."

~:~

Where others see complexity, the person of
action sees the thing that needs to be done.

~:~

Pay attention to what needs to be done—
not to what should have been done.

~:~

If you are doing your best there is plenty to do.

~:~

Always get up on the right side of bed.

~:~

Your life has a Start Menu, just like Windows.

~:~

Self-compassion, but never self-pity.

∼:∼

Let my spirit rise above this sea of negativity.

∼:∼

A fearful person lives on Planet Scary.

∼:∼

If your eyes are open there is plenty to see.

∼:∼

Your thirst can never be satisfied
if your glass is always half empty.

∼:∼

A pessimist believes that everything is
for the worse—and there is nothing
worse than being a pessimist.

∼:∼

ATTITUDE

Just tell your neurotic inner voice to shut up.

~:~

A light heart is young until the day it stops.

~:~

A bad attitude can be spotted from a mile away.

~:~

Be useful, keeping in mind that
complaining is not useful.

~:~

Every day of my life—
this incredible adventure!

~:~

3

A good cook is adventurous—
a great cook is insane.

∾:∾

Try to weigh yourself on a day
when gravity is not too high.

∾:∾

The body arrives in front of the refrigerator
and the door opens by some mysterious means.

∾:∾

Food is delicious in inverse proportion
to its health benefits.

∾:∾

I am always amazed at what I just ate.

∾:∾

The good news is that I love to cook—
the bad news is that I look it.

∾:∾

Prove that eating broccoli extended my life
by a year and I might do it, but if it was
only a month, it wouldn't be worth it.

~:~

"Fast food"—the very words give me indigestion.

~:~

Does the world exist before
I have my first cup of coffee?

~:~

You can't talk seriously about food
with a skinny person.

~:~

Dinner should be a leisurely journey to dessert.

~:~

There are more people in the world
who eat insects than who eat truffles.

~:~

Don't expect to find a great lover in
someone who is not interested in food.

~:~

There isn't always sex,
but there is always chocolate.

~:~

Vegetarians occupy the high moral ground,
but my stomach is not a moralist.

~:~

An oyster is the only thing that a
civilized person swallows alive.

~:~

A vegetarian and a cannibal can agree
that no animals should be harmed
in making their dinners.

~:~

We didn't get to the top of the
food chain by eating broccoli.

~:~

The pleasure of eating something awful,
like a snail, is in the sauce.

~:~

I will die happy if I outlive some of the people
who keep telling me that my diet is unhealthy.

~:~

Food is love, but love is not sugar-free and fat-free.

~:~

If the pig knew why it was being fattened
it would lose its appetite.

~:~

Open your best bottle and cook the chicken in the
wine that you were planning to drink it with.

~:~

I can't control my weight because
I'm constantly being attacked by food.

~:~

The secret ingredient is usually ketchup.

~:~

Any wine worth drinking
goes well with chocolate.

~:~

The pot calls the kettle black, and the teakettle
calls the pot dull-witted, and the saucepan
calls the teakettle shrill, and the skillet
calls the saucepan rude, and the casserole calls
the skillet hot-tempered, and the kettle calls
the casserole stodgy.

~:~

Resist the urge to babble when there is a
lull in the dinner-party conversation.

~:~

Antacids make the eating of many
wonderful things possible.

~:~

You will tire of eating lobster before
you will tire of eating French fries.

~:~

In the poised young smoker I see the
old woman gasping for breath.

~::~

It's easier to accumulate flesh than money.

~::~

If you are looking for symptoms,
you will find plenty of them.

~::~

I prefer to see a healthy-looking doctor.

~::~

You can't drop a tattoo off at the
thrift shop when it goes out of style.

~::~

Our glands produce hormones long before
our brains begin to produce intelligence.

~::~

If I walked to the gym I wouldn't need it so much.

∾:∾

Alcohol is a preservative, but not for brains.

∾:∾

It is not human nature not to worry.

∾:∾

Nervous people make me nervous.

∾:∾

If you want to hear something profound,
don't ask a wino.

∾:∾

People who love people drive carefully.

∾:∾

Football is hard bodies colliding on the screen
and soft ones sinking into the sofa.

∾:∾

Middle age is when you grow your middle.

∾:∾

Your body is a temple given to you by God—
defile it and you will receive Biblical punishments.

∾:∾

Eventually a hypochondriac dies,
to everyone's amazement.

∾:∾

Crazy people are only a little crazier.

∾:∾

At some point in the evening
you realize that you are asleep.

∾:∾

Surviving a serious illness puts
everything on the table.

∾:∾

When we are children the world can be a scary
place, but as we grow older it is our body
that is the scary place.

∾:∾

One of the benefits of growing older is
that you get a lot of extra skin.

∼:∼

The meat industry puts hormones in our beef and
the drug industry puts hormones in our women.

∼:∼

When you're on a diet,
food will leap into your mouth.

∼:∼

Weight is a boomerang; it just keeps coming back.

∼:∼

The most carcinogenic substance
you are exposed to is sunlight.

∼:∼

You get fat in the moments between when you
know you should stop and when you do.

∼:∼

I only allow myself dessert on special
occasions—and what occasion is not special?

∼:∼

HEALTH

Let yourself be inebriated by nothing, except life.

∼:∼

Does the proverb "Physician, heal thyself"
apply to psychologists?

∼:∼

Addictions crowd out other interests.

∼:∼

Don't eat anything with a lot of
small print on the package.

∼:∼

God, moving in his mysterious ways,
seems to be fattening us.

∼:∼

My country 'tis obese.

∼:∼

A cocktail is a very pretty drug.

∼:∼

Exercise may not make us thinner, live longer, or prevent cancer—but it does make us feel virtuous.

∼:∼

How did Gluttony become
more popular than Lust?

∼:∼

Your mother taught you how to eat,
but she didn't teach you how to stop.

∼:∼

A psychologist will interpret a dream
of looking for a bathroom without
asking if you woke up having to pee.

∼:∼

When we can't find our car, we worry that it has
been stolen—and when we do find it, we worry
that we are losing our minds.

∼:∼

The office guys in the gym now have bigger
muscles than the factory guys in the bar.

∼:∼

When you accept that you control nothing
in the world except your own behavior,
life becomes much less complicated.

∾:∾

Don't fuss.

∾:∾

It is always easy to make your life difficult.

∾:∾

We are the fishermen who weave the nets that
ensnare us.

∾:∾

It is in a rare moment of complete clarity
that one makes a major life decision.

∾:∾

Don't let your life story be all fish that got away.

∾:∾

There are three halves to
anything that is done by halves.

∾:∾

Each day brings a new problem, and a previous
day's crisis solves itself without your intervention.

∾:∾

Life is a challenge—if you enjoy picking fights.

∾:∾

A few words can contain the design for a life.

∾:∾

Don't offer philosophy when hearing of tragedy.

∾:∾

A successful person feels a little less
a failure than the rest of us.

∾:∾

Trying to be "philosophical" about a
disaster in your life is small consolation.

∾:∾

Looking back on my life, I wonder if there
is someone who shares a regret with me.

∼:∼

Other people can make us sad, but only we
can make ourselves truly miserable.

∼:∼

With prosperity and leisure comes the luxury
of being able to make problems for ourselves.

∼:∼

If you have made more good decisions than bad
ones, you have had a better-than-average life.

∼:∼

We often know the answer to one of life's
questions, but we are afraid to ask the question.

∼:∼

Having a major setback in life
tells you what you are made of.

∼:∼

We change long before we realize
that we have changed.

~:~

If you must be a loser in life, try to be a good loser.

~:~

We divide our time between the universe that
exists and another that exists only
in our imagination.

~:~

There is no brotherhood of all mankind,
but there might be a sisterhood.

~:~

You have as much work to do
on your life as in your work.

~:~

There is just enough time in the moment before
we ski into the tree to regret our indecisiveness.

~:~

First we play, then we work, then we play again.

~:~

In the time it takes to read this a
multitude of lives have begun and ended.

~:~

If you are completely organized, you
probably don't have time for much else.

~:~

A happy life can be the result of a
determination to be happy and to
ignore the usual neurotic thoughts.

~:~

Birthdays are milestones in
what we have not accomplished.

~:~

One becomes an adult by an
abrupt series of discoveries.

~:~

Freedom is the ability to decide
what you are going to do today.

~:~

For best results examine your life
frequently and adjust as necessary.

~:~

We who live in the slow lane like
seeing empty pages in our calendars.

~:~

I may be a product of my circumstances, but
I refuse to live my life under such limitations.

~:~

The road not taken was not your path.

~:~

There is no ego too large
to fit into a standard grave.

∼:∼

What would you like to be remembered for?

∼:∼

Many small things annoy you—
take comfort in how much less annoying
they will be when you are dead.

∼:∼

What is your hurry?
You know where your journey ends.

∼:∼

You can't call a dead person and
tell her how much you love her.

∼:∼

I only ask you to remember me dancing.

∼:∼

When I die I would like people to say,
"He was a good listener."

∼:∼

If you plan to confess some great secret
on your deathbed, do it a little before
you lose the ability to speak.

∼:∼

Death is the hardest truth;
all the others are bearable.

∼:∼

The man who is acting most naturally
is at his own funeral.

∼:∼

Suicide is the last word on the subject.

∼:∼

DEATH

At least let me put my photos
in the album before I croak.

∾:∾

The hardest universe to imagine is
one in which we do not exist.

∾:∾

A great pleasure is the cessation of pain.

∾:∾

If you are comfortable with death you have
one less major problem to deal with in life.

∾:∾

When I'm dead I won't care what people say
about me—so why should I wait to
not care until I'm dead?

∾:∾

The widower is more likely to
be merry than the widow.

∾:∾

Write something about yourself on your photos
so your descendants will know who you were.

∼:∼

There is one piece of bad news that
you don't have to worry about hearing,
because it will be about you.

∼:∼

A consolation of becoming very elderly is knowing
that your passing will not cause so much pain.

∼:∼

My only protection is in this constant worry.

∼:∼

Achieving a posthumous reputation
proves that death is no glass ceiling.

∼:∼

Let your life story have a happy ending.

∼:∼

I just noticed that I got old,
right after I was young.

∽:∽

Really nice people generally have time to stop and
visit—it seems that the universe allots them more
time.

∽:∽

There is no time and place more interesting
than the time and place you are at now.

∽:∽

At what age does one discover that it is
possible to sit quietly?

∽:∽

The older you get, the fewer excuses you need.

∽:∽

All good things must come to an end—
but not all mediocre things.

∽:∽

The hardest thing to do gracefully is age.

~:~

I'm too old to argue.

~:~

Today you have a day less than you had
yesterday—did you spend it wisely?

~:~

An hour is not so long—neither is a lifetime.

~:~

It is our oldest feature that betrays our real age.

~:~

To have a sense of history is to know how
quickly one's generation slips into oblivion.

~:~

Don't tell me what I should have done
differently, I'm no time traveler.

~:~

Our age is the constant against which
we measure that of our friends: who looks
younger than we do, and who seems older.

~:~

If you wish to call attention to your age,
complain about all your aches and pains.

~:~

Thirty years ago I could do cartwheels—
now I can do mental ones.

~:~

If you still have all the ideals of your youth forty
years later, you are probably some kind of nut.

~:~

Passing a mirror… who is that weird old person?

~:~

Your past is not an excuse for your present.

~:~

Curmudgeons do not improve with age.

~:~

If you are well fed, and you get old,
eventually you will look like an owl.

∼:∼

There is no beauty greater than graceful old age.

∼:∼

I have a lot of mileage on me—am I entitled
to an upgrade on my life journey?

∼:∼

The older people get, the more
they have in common.

∼:∼

Why do I waste time? Because it can't be recycled.

∼:∼

It is not true that everyone has the same
amount of time—some people have more
time in an hour than others have in a week.

∼:∼

Tomorrow is far more interesting than yesterday.

∼:∼

TIME

One day is like another, and yet each day
unfolds with its own unique logic.

∽:∽

"Ageless" is a nice way of saying really, really old.

∽:∽

A few minutes in a doctor's
waiting room is about an hour.

∽:∽

Try to spend more quality time with yourself.

∽:∽

What is written in stone will be erased by geology.

∽:∽

True success is not having to
account for your time to anyone.

∽:∽

There is so much to do, and we only
have a moment out of eternity....

∽:∽

People who know nothing
are the first to say, "I know."

~:~

If you would just reverse that opinion slightly I
would be in complete agreement with you.

~:~

The heart is the most intelligent organ.

~:~

We are only passengers driven
by our restless minds.

~:~

I forgive all my teachers for what I don't know.

~:~

Wise men are often to be found at home,
the world having no use for them.

~:~

This world is far more interesting than anything
that could happen merely inside my head.

~:~

I am contemplating my navel,
and find it rather deep.

~:~

It must be consoling to be a philosopher,
when things go wrong in your life.

~:~

I am pretty sure that I am right about something.

~:~

If I were an ant, the grain of salt with which
I take your opinion would be a boulder.

~:~

An intellectual tends to see complexities
where they do not actually exist.

~:~

The mind can also become constipated.

~:~

That's my opinion, I read it somewhere.

∼:∼

What was I thinking when I was so thoughtless?

∼:∼

The wisdom of the ages is sitting on a barstool, but
the future is being mapped in a coffeehouse.

∼:∼

People often elevate mere prejudices
to "a philosophy."

∼:∼

There is no school of philosophy that
approaches ordinary common sense.

∼:∼

Most of what is useful in life is known
only to a small minority of alert listeners.

∼:∼

If you have thought about the issues and formed
your own opinion you are equal to any pundit.

∼:∼

I have a hundred things
on my mind and not much in it.

~:~

Original thinkers are irritating because they insert
a grain of sand under the shell of our complacency.

~:~

Don't expect a keen exchange of opinion
with someone who has a dull ax to grind.

~:~

Let me think about that for… a few years.

~:~

An authority on everything is
an authority on nothing.

~:~

If you could sum up everything you've learned,
and then subtract everything you're not
sure about, what would the remainder be?

~:~

Now that I am old and wise
I might learn something.

⁓:⁓

Sometimes we turn on the radio because silence
would leave us alone with our troubled thoughts.

⁓:⁓

The good teacher always has a smart class and the
bad teacher always has a dumb one.

⁓:⁓

Some people learn everything they need to know
in kindergarten, others in traffic school.

⁓:⁓

You can't take bullshit by the horns.

⁓:⁓

Like a bee that buzzes from flower to flower,
the mind buzzes from thought to thought.

⌒:⌒

That's what I said, but not what I meant,
such is my poverty of language.

⌒:⌒

A person who is generally miserable
can still become a great philosopher.

⌒:⌒

You don't have to be a great thinker
to be a thoughtful person.

⌒:⌒

Given the choice, how many men would choose a
very large brain and a very small penis over a very
small brain and a very large penis?

⌒:⌒

First thought, best thought—
last thought, also best thought.

⌒:⌒

Gaining control of your thoughts is as easy as
sitting by the ocean and controlling the waves.

∼:∼

Because I am a genius,
I only need to use half my wit.

∼:∼

Real ideas have exactness,
but nonsense is always vague.

∼:∼

If you really have something to say,
plain language will do.

∼:∼

Don't give advice without first
asking if advice is wanted.

∼:∼

Philosophy is about how to live, but the lives of the
great philosophers provide few useful role models.

∼:∼

Love is the main event.

∼:∼

I'll be your world, if you'll be my mine.

∼:∼

Never forget that you are married to a very
beautiful woman.

∼:∼

True love does not need a lot of space.

∼:∼

A love affair becomes a relationship
when someone says "We…."

∼:∼

Lovers are a world.

∼:∼

We can exist without love,
but we can't live without it.

∼:∼

Was I really in love with that snake?

∽:∽

Sexy, sex, ex—it was a brief affair.

∽:∽

You can't buy love, but people
spend a lot of money trying.

∽:∽

How can our relationship grow when
you don't respect my need to discuss
everything that is wrong with you?

∽:∽

Love begins with attraction, which is
the great mystery of our physiology.

∽:∽

A single kiss can change your life.

∽:∽

Memory has a special place for first times.

∽:∽

Falling in love is the second best thing in life;
knowing that it will always last is the best.

~:~

Whichever sex you are, the mystery of the
opposite one keeps life interesting.

~:~

Don't waste your time trying
to warm up a cold fish.

~:~

There is a hundred times more sex
in the world than lovemaking.

~:~

A cult leader creates a community with his
charisma and destroys it with his libido.

~:~

Some men are only capable of
real intercourse after lovemaking.

~:~

If you sleep with people who have troubles,
you will certainly catch them.

~:~

The sexual athlete begins his game
by serving an absolutely great opening line.

~:~

An unhappy couple fools no one.

~:~

If your heart is big enough the world can fit inside
of it.

~:~

Sleeping alone is not even good for sleeping.

~:~

Our first reaction to being jilted is
that it must be some kind of mistake.

~:~

It is possible to be in love with someone
you really don't like all that much.

~:~

Money is sexy—but the less sexy you are,
the more money it takes to make you so.

~:~

Sex is slowly parting ways with reproduction.

~:~

A first date is not grounds for an interrogation.

~:~

After spending years finding the perfect mate
we find that we are incapable of perfect mating.

~:~

The moon is more flattering than
any lighting arranged by experts.

~:~

Forget anything your friends
would rather you forgot.

∼:∼

We value people we have known for a long
time—because they prove we have a past.

∼:∼

When people talk about total loyalty,
they are talking about a dog.

∼:∼

Insulting a friend is like pouring
a herbicide on your garden.

∼:∼

We are in danger of forgetting our friends
when our lives are going exceptionally well.

∼:∼

We call our numerous acquaintances friends,
but one is blessed to have even a few true friends.

∼:∼

Duration inflates the value of friendships.

∼:∼

If you have youthful friends who are dissatisfied
and unhappy, expect to endure their bitterness
and grudges as they grow older.

∼:∼

Many generous people would die before
they would ask a friend for help.

∼:∼

We know enough not to rub a cat
the wrong way, but not a person.

∼:∼

You get more mileage from
alcohol in good company.

∼:∼

When we say someone is a "real character"
we are not talking about character.

∼:∼

We often ask for advice when
the last thing we want is advice.

∼:∼

How could anyone not like me,
when I'm so charming?

∼:∼

A man tells the joke but forgets the punch line, a
woman tells the punch line but forgets the joke.

∼:∼

We sometimes find ourselves in a place where
everyone looks like someone we know,
but no one is.

~:~

An interesting conversation is like two people
holding an object and turning it in their hands to
view all sides.

~:~

When we visit very old friends we are
young together for a few hours.

~:~

A real conversation, which is something rare,
is a series of linked statements.

~:~

Make friends with people who enlarge your world.

~:~

When home is a happy place,
one is happy to be at home.

~:~

There is plenty to do at home, without going out
and causing more problems in the world.

~:~

We invite a stranger to make himself comfortable
in the living room we never set foot in.

~:~

One day something in the garage
will prove to be useful.

~:~

It is impossible to paint a room the
exact color you had in mind.

~:~

Real hospitality is being invited
to eat in the kitchen, like family.

~:~

My home is always as neat as a pin—
five minutes before the company arrives.

~:~

Most Americans couldn't describe the place
where they live because it is a vast,
incomprehensible, suburban sprawl.

~:~

We may be the preeminent world power,
but I'm not even a regional power at home.

~:~

Suburban life is boring and pleasant and safe,
and that suits most Americans just fine.

~:~

Homeless people have often
thrown away a few homes.

~:~

There is no such thing as a clean house,
from the viewpoint of a microbiologist, an
allergist, a health inspector, an environmental
chemist, or your mother.

~:~

An old house is moody in bad weather,
creaking and sighing.

~:~

What am I doing this weekend?
Must I always be doing?

~:~

Your house is thinking,
"These people too shall pass."

~:~

A walk around a suburban subdivision
with cul-de-sacs is a walk to nowhere.

∾:∾

At a certain age we say, "I will live out
my days in this place."

∾:∾

The true gardener can no more relax in her garden
than a farmer would relax in his field of corn.

∾:∾

Marry someone who reads instructions.

~:~

Just the sight of a happy family is therapeutic.

~:~

Children want nothing more than they
want their parents to love each other.

~:~

Women look for husbands far more
than men look for wives.

~:~

The histories of most families are
writ in a garage full of junk.

~:~

I have six billion cousins, but I am only on
speaking terms with a few hundred of them.

~:~

Don't forget that family stories
are mostly just stories.

～:～

Finding just the right gift is a gift.

～:～

In marriage, it is better to be wrong because
being right is the right to remain celibate.

～:～

Dating is fun until you start doing it with
intentions—then it becomes nerve-wracking.

～:～

An unhappy marriage is already a separation.

～:～

The worst part of divorce is knowing that
you will have to go through dating again.

～:～

She only wanted to marry money and
that's why money did not want to marry her.

∽:∼

The only thing that is seldom contested
in a divorce is the wedding album.

∽:∼

The course that is a mandatory prerequisite to
all further education is called Toilet Training.

∽:∼

If you are a good parent your children will
make their own mistakes, but not yours.

∽:∼

My kids have difficulties; other people's kids
have problems.

∽:∼

There is nothing more embarrassing to a teenager
than having parents and being seen with them.

~:~

Resentment is one of the privileges of privilege.

~:~

You can blame your parents for your childhood,
but don't blame them for your adulthood.

~:~

It's a lot easier to start a family feud
than to stop one.

~:~

Have you ever heard a father telling his thirty-year-
old son, "I'm worried that you aren't married yet"?

~:~

Monogamy often flourishes when
the field has been sown with wild oats.

~:~

Our obligations to our children
are reversed in old age.

∼:∼

Relationships built on obligation
are always grudging.

∼:∼

Sometimes the opposite of no is still no.

∼:∼

Your parents didn't think you had any sense,
and theirs felt the same way about them.

∼:∼

It's the thought that counts, but
a thoughtful present counts more.

∼:∼

Let your parents come to live with you,
but never go to live with your parents.

∼:∼

Before responding to provocation,
take a breath and count to a thousand.

∾:∾

Look at this terrible wound I have made
out of a small slight!

∾:∾

"Make Love, Not War," sounded
pretty good to me, so I did.

∾:∾

To find the right person, become the right person.

∾:∾

With marriage, sometimes it
takes a few tries to get it right.

∾:∾

Ninety-eight percent of social engagements
are arranged by wives, the other
two percent are unaccounted for.

∾:∾

The intimacies of a Wednesday-night poker game
can outlast those of the player's marriages.

∼:∼

Pray to a saint, but never marry one.

∼:∼

After a certain age all the single men
seem to disappear.

∼:∼

The most complicated of all contracts
is the marriage contract.

∼:∼

Sometimes even an adult needs
to be told when to go to bed.

∼:∼

We must learn to walk on our own twice.

∼:∼

As a marriage matures, the number of understandings, agreements, and treaties multiplies, as between nations at peace.

~:~

The youngest child wears the oldest clothes.

~:~

A happy family is of little interest to novelists, psychologists, or other experts in dysfunction.

~:~

The latest form of child abuse is heavy scheduling.

~:~

The child whose needs are unmet becomes the adult whose needs can never be met.

~:~

A marriage that goes on the rocks can still take a long time to sink.

~:~

A man stays in touch with society
by means of a wife.

~:~

You must decipher the rules of the
family that you marry into.

~:~

The most incompetent of parents began
their work by producing a perfect baby.

~:~

When you have small children,
ten percent of your life is personal.

~:~

One job, one house, one wife—
believe it or not, it does happen.

~:~

Babies do not negotiate.

~:~

Affection will bring more forgiveness
than explanations.

~:~

A woman can try on two outfits faster
than a man can put on a shirt.

~:~

She told her friends about her serious relationship
and he told his about his new girlfriend.

~:~

The sleepy woman is trying to go to sleep—
the sleepy man is already asleep.

~:~

A woman will never forgive another woman
for a careless remark about her weight or age.

~:~

A woman worries about the aging of her entire
body, and a man about only a small part.

~:~

Men celebrate their birthdays,
while women recover from them.

~:~

If a man likes being a leader, the best place
to do it is on the dance floor.

~:~

A man sees a tiny wrinkle
where a woman sees a chasm.

~:~

"We need to talk" is an invitation
to a most unpleasant conversation.

~:~

There is no goddess skinny enough
to work as a fashion model.

~:~

A cross is very pretty when
displayed in décolletage.

~:~

Dating becomes a relationship
when asking becomes assuming.

~:~

When I see an attractive young woman
with a dreadful tattoo I lose all confidence
in any notion of human progress.

~:~

We worry about losing our memory,
yet there are things we wish we could forget.

∾∶∾

Share your thoughts, not your memoirs.

∾∶∾

As adults we remember far more than
ever happened during our childhood.

∾∶∾

The great joy of an old-timer is telling
a newcomer how great it was twenty years ago.

∾∶∾

If you can remember the names and faces of a
thousand people you are presidential timber.

∾∶∾

Who cares what you did twenty years ago?
What matters is what you are doing now.

~::~

You can't build memories out of daydreams.

~::~

Don't schlep your past everywhere.

~::~

There are people who tell the story of their life
over and over again until they come to believe it.

~::~

My childhood memories of the verdant smells of
nature are more vivid than anything my nose is
able to detect now.

~::~

A chess master has a tremendous gift
that is perfectly useless.

~::~

Leave the sleeping dogs
of your past to their slumbers.

~:~

You are never really alone with your thoughts,
because so many voices and faces crowd into them.

~:~

A tattoo is a way of keeping alive the
memory of being young and stupid.

~:~

The mind travels most smoothly in well-worn ruts.

~:~

Those who have taken a walk on the wild side in
their youth have a certain gleam in their eyes.

~:~

There was once a distinction
between famous and infamous.

~:~

The echo of crime is the slamming
of a prison-cell door.

~:~

The truth is always the simple version.

~:~

A prude is generally a very dirty-minded person.

~:~

Most of us would rather lose the
manuscript of our entire past than
have certain chapters published.

~:~

The most skillful liar is one who is able to
persuade himself of the truth of his lie.

∼:∼

To avoid complications, tell the truth
or change the subject.

∼:∼

Morality is like quicksand:
one sinks more easily than one rises.

∼:∼

A skillful liar begins with the truth
and then works in tints and shadings.

∼:∼

More loose behavior is prevented by the
fear of gossip than by morality, law,
and religion combined.

∼:∼

Poor people go to jail from rage,
rich people from greed.

~:~

A public defender is hardly defending the public.

~:~

There is about the same amount of depravity
everywhere—the only difference being that
there are places in which it is on display.

~:~

It takes character to be a good poker
player—deceitful, calculating, and secretive
character.

~:~

Forty years of feminism—
and still those stupid shoes.

~:~

How could you have ever thought that I actually
wanted your honest opinion of how I look?

~:~

To be vain, first pretend that you are attractive.

~:~

Don't brag about your possessions,
they are only yours for a little while.

~:~

As we fuss over a tiny spot on our pants,
somewhere in a very poor country a man is
attempting to cover his nakedness with a tattered
rag that once was pants.

~:~

If you think your possessions are valuable,
try holding a yard sale.

~:~

Vain does not see vanity.

~:~

There are no immortal words.

~:~

I am extremely proud of my humility
and my modesty.

~:~

We like to believe that we are
better looking than our photos.

~:~

There is no beauty with a sour expression.

~:~

As gravity pulls you to the earth,
so vanity pulls you to the mirror.

∾:∾

An improvement in the manufacture of mirrors
is also an advancement in vanity.

∾:∾

An important person vanishes,
consumed by his own importance.

∾:∾

We find our own skin more fascinating
than any abstract painting.

∾:∾

Honestly, suppose you had to choose
between becoming sexier or becoming smarter?

∾:∾

An oversized ego is like tight pants on a big butt.

∾:∾

VANITY

Try not to frown when you
are considering something.

∾:∾

Vanity is more durable than beauty.

∾:∾

Give that aging sexpot lots of credit for trying.

∾:∾

You say that you aren't vain—
so try going an entire day without saying "I."

∾:∾

We ask the mirror not if we are the fairest in
the land, but if we are still even a little bit sexy.

∾:∾

Now that you are famous—so what?

∾:∾

White comes in pink to tan,
and black comes in tan to ebony.

~:~

A culture has as much will to live as a species has.

~:~

Cultures are most interesting where they intersect.

~:~

The Midwest is flat and the people there
are more levelheaded.

~:~

There are people who have a gift for
looking distinguished, and nothing more.

~:~

We carry our ethnic heritage
like an invisible costume.

~:~

We attach more importance to skin color
than to hair or eye color because we are racists.

∾:∾

America is divided between those
who love lawns and those who love grass.

∾:∾

Working class is when you take better care
of your car than of your body.

∾:∾

Half of what we brought from Europe
deserved to be left behind as fast as possible.

∾:∾

The weaker the culture,
the more it fears intermarriage.

∾:∾

The white person who gets nicely tanned
on a Third-World beach would still
not care to be mistaken for a native.

∼:∼

You can hear worse language on a golf course
than at a boxing match.

∼:∼

We ask people about their ethnic origins
and then we foolishly think that
we know something about them.

∼:∼

We love and cherish the immigrants we know,
and hate and fear the ones we don't know.

∼:∼

Heaven is a place where
there is plenty of work to do.

~:~

The prayers of an atheist
have a special charm to God.

~:~

After my enlightenment—ask me then.

~:~

One spark can burn a forest—
one divine spark can transform a life.

~:~

Religion reminds us that we
can be better than we are.

~:~

It was a great sermon—
I stayed awake almost until the end.

~:~

Faith in religion is possible just as arithmetic
exists and is useful, even though numbers
are entirely imagined.

∾:∾

Anyone who has a conception
of God is a theologian.

∾:∾

New-Age people do not have
anything exactly in mind.

∾:∾

The problem of evil sticks in the
craw of religion like a fishbone.

∾:∾

Safer to put your faith in religion
than in the stock market.

∾:∾

If you like to take chances with your faith,
ask your spiritual leader a political question.

∾:∾

I climbed a mountain and I saw God—
or could it have been the altitude?

∾:∾

Money can easily be raised to build a
magnificent house of worship; filling it with
worshipers is a more difficult matter.

∾:∾

A religion can run on even ten percent faith.

∾:∾

The leaders of all great religions have but
one thing in common: funny hats.

∾:∾

I'll be happy to see anyone,
assuming there is an afterlife.

∾:∾

If you would like your prayers to be granted,
pray that you should become a better person.

∾:∾

Some faiths require a bigger leap .... of faith.

~:~

The Jews have ten thousand popes, all infallible.

~:~

If the answer to any spiritual question is readily
provided, you are in the presence of a charlatan.

~:~

Through meditation I have discovered
that I am my mind's slave.

~:~

God's idea of hilarious would be
a conversation with a theologian.

~:~

In a hundred years there will be a world culture,
and in a thousand years there will be a world race,
but there will never be one world religion.

~:~

The Bible is tribal.

~:~

Has anyone noticed that the Crusades
occur every thousand years?

~:~

God tells every religion that it is his favorite.

~:~

Fully observing any religion would
leave little time for anything else.

~:~

Nonviolence works well against pacifists.

∾:∾

Military discipline enables an army facing a
superior enemy to contemplate its impending
destruction with equanimity.

∾:∾

We are taught to believe in our
system of government, whatever that is.

∾:∾

It is best not to come to the attention
of the government.

∾:∾

God may be on our side, but He is not
always in a mood to play.

∾:∾

Our faith in democracy is shaken
by the election of a complete fool.

~:~

Medals are given only for murders
committed in uniform.

~:~

Your legal lifestyle rests comfortably
on the shoulders of illegal immigrants.

~:~

The Right hates minorities
and the Left hates the country.

~:~

Majorities are generally not too fond of minorities.

~:~

No one is entitled to anything more
than a decent opportunity.

~:~

There are an infinite number of societies in any
society, and they can barely conceive of each other.

~:~

The armies of democracies
tend to hold their ground.

~:~

Compared to the behavior of nations,
I declare myself sane.

~:~

To improve your wind for running,
pretend that you are a politician.

~:~

If it is very good or very bad,
it probably originated in California.

~:~

Would you listen to a radio station
that reported only good news?

~:~

The efficiency of a government agency
can be too small to measure.

∾:∾

I have arranged the map of the world
to keep my coffee cup and my gas tank full.

∾:∾

Politics is a much rougher game than football.

∾:∾

We like the police to be handy—but not too close.

∾:∾

Discuss politics only with people who always vote.

∾:∾

A government that doesn't provide healthcare
for its citizens is hardly worth the price.

∾:∾

A nation of homeowners is more concerned
with lawns than with politics.

∾:∾

One begins a legal dispute with
an irrational belief in justice.

∼:∼

What was thought to be a conspiracy usually
turns out to be a major instance of stupidity.

∼:∼

Congress tends to resemble itself more
than it resembles the country.

∼:∼

In politics, as in ancient Rome,
the knife is still placed in the back.

∼:∼

I have not encountered any form of taxation
that comes with representation.

∼:∼

Everyone who sees action in war
is to some extent a casualty.

∼:∼

The Constitution is mostly a matter
of interpretation, like the Bible.

∼:∼

The budget is always cut so as to cause
the most pain, in order to reconcile
the citizens to the next tax increase.

∼:∼

We were told we were winning the Vietnam War
until the last Americans were helicoptered
off the roof of the embassy.

∼:∼

The preppie millionaire is coached to speak
like a workin' man when he run for office.

∼:∼

"One nation, indivisible" — except by race,
ethnicity, region, politics, class,
religion, age, and gender.

∼:∼

The left always venerates the working class,
a love that is seldom reciprocated.

∼:∼

The President of the United States —
our disposable monarch.

∼:∼

Ten dollars an hour on one side of the fence,
ten dollars a day on the other —
would the fence stop you?

∼:∼

Paranoia is the default mentality
of the far left and the far right.

∼:∼

The American brain is not sufficiently evolved
to grasp the duplicities of the Middle East.

∼:∼

I can't say I have much to show
for my lifetime of voting.

∼:∼

Any kind of weather will do
if you are an indoorsy person.

~:~

If you truly want to preserve the wilderness,
stay home.

~:~

On a beautiful day you can bathe in the air.

~:~

A brilliant conversationalist falls silent
at the rim of the Grand Canyon.

~:~

In California the weather is wonderful,
but people complain about it just as much.

~:~

Nature is primarily engaged in a devouring.

~:~

Mankind is warlike because we are all descended
from fierce warriors—if they had not been fierce,
our ancestors would not have survived.

∽:∽

There is no landscape made by man that
surpasses any landscape not made by man.

∽:∽

Humans are the only species that can
love another species more than their own.

∽:∽

An ant doesn't look like it knows
where it's going, but it does.

∽:∽

Country people seldom say that they are looking
forward to getting away to the city for a weekend.

∽:∽

Being in nature is very tiring—
afterwards I must have a long nap.

∽:∽

A tree makes a good living on
water and carbon dioxide.

~:~

Nature is always beautiful if you are a
human—the rest of creation is looking for
other creatures to eat.

~:~

If I were my cat I would know what I want in life.

~:~

In the history of the earth, anything
that lives on land is a newcomer.

~:~

A cat has boundaries.

~:~

My backyard is wilderness enough.

~:~

A forest makes a very good neighbor.

~:~

As the top predator, we have the luxury of being
able to linger over the carcass at our dinner.

∼:∼

We rule nature, but we are ruled by our natures.

∼:∼

The next age of mankind will be
the Age of Consequences.

∼:∼

The Gray-haired Woman has
become an endangered species.

∼:∼

A cat has an entire beauty salon in her tongue.

∼:∼

An environmentalist in the boardroom
is worth two in the bush.

∼:∼

A dog has just enough consciousness
to be anxious.

∼:∼

The herring can no more conceive that it is
going to be pickled in a jar than we can
conceive that we are made out of herring

~:~

If you really considered what is involved
in walking on two legs you would hardly
be able to stand up.

~:~

Global warming is global karma.

~:~

Nothing is possible
that goes against human nature.

~:~

When you have poison oak
you love nature a little less.

~:~

In our own backyards, we are all NIMBYs.

~:~

Every day of my life, a major discovery.

∼:∼

God-fearing man is being replaced
by Science-fearing man.

∼:∼

Physics is becoming more improbable
than religion.

∼:∼

The human mind is more like a kaleidoscope
than a microscope or a telescope.

∼:∼

Gravity gets me down.

∼:∼

Sometimes a mere probability is
promoted to a proof.

∼:∼

I was born in the Atomic Age
and I will die in the Technology Age.

∾:∾

All we see is the skin of the onion.

∾:∾

If someone has a new idea and you
instantly offer an objection, you are
part of the problem, not the solution.

∾:∾

More problems are solved by tinkering
than by brilliance.

∾:∾

Thanks to rapid advances in technology,
for the first time in history we are no longer able
to fix anything.

∾:∾

Most problems are manageable if you
can just think of something to try.

∾:∾

If you enjoy banging your head on your desk, I suggest not backing up your computer files.

~:~

Psychology proves the danger of applying theories about human nature to real life.

~:~

Economists can now predict the past with great accuracy.

~:~

Open a bag of your favorite potato chips and you will begin to believe in the concept of perpetual motion.

~:~

A genius is someone who has had at least one truly original thought during his lifetime.

~:~

Freud left a fog over psychology that is just beginning to lift; Jung left a primordial swamp.

~:~

What Hegel and Marx called the dialectic
is actually the mind of a neurotic, in which
everything calls up its opposite and a negation.

∾∶∽

In the final struggle,
we will not rule nature, nature will rule us.

∾∶∽

Technology enables us to always
be in touch without ever touching.

∾∶∽

Breaking up requires a lot of deleting.

∾∶∽

Unlikely coincidences occur frequently because
the number of things that could occur is
practically infinite.

∾∶∽

We live in the Age of Technology—
but most of us don't have a clue.

∾∶∽

The toothpaste is never empty,
we just get tired of squeezing the tube.

∾:∾

Our brains are running software
that is two million years old.

∾:∾

We are losing the war against microbes because
their adaptability trumps our intelligence.

∾:∾

We no longer know if the consumers drive the
technology or the technology
drives the consumers.

∾:∾

The Internet is a city in which a
bad neighborhood can appear on any corner.

∾:∾

If we had decent fur we might not
have invented fire.

∾:∾

The marketplace may be efficient,
but no one has ever said that it is kind.

~:~

Try to get customer service and
you will see that we live in Babel.

~:~

The ego rapidly expands to fill the larger office.

~:~

A sinking economy causes fear—
and fear sinks the economy.

~:~

It is hard to maintain equanimity
when you have just lost a lot of money.

~:~

A dull business meeting gets a lot more interesting
when you realize that your job is on the line.

~:~

The theory that customers will put up
with anything is called "voicemail."

~:~

Watching a televangelist at work
confirms my faith in the free market.

~:~

Expert opinions are bought and
sold like any other commodity.

~:~

To play the game you must either
know the rules or make the rules.

~:~

That banks are eager to lend you money
should be warning enough.

~:~

Being self-employed is a modern way
of saying that you live by your wits.

~:~

A thing is obviously worth what it sells for—but
this is only true at the moment of the transaction.

~:~

How many who curse spam
have ever tasted Spam?

~:~

A sales force is motivated by greed
and driven by fear.

~:~

All advertising is spam.

~:~

The only kind of snake you can trust
is the kind that crawls on the ground.

~:~

One of the triumphs of capitalism
was turning "shop" into a verb.

~:~

Companies take booths at trade shows
to prove that they exist.

~:~

Ambition is always naked,
because there is no way to clothe it.

~:~

An Indian casino is where the white man
goes to get scalped.

~:~

There is nothing less entertaining
than business entertainment.

~:~

The answer to almost any
legal question is expensive.

~:~

In a country lacking an aristocracy,
money does the job nicely.

∾:∾

If you are wondering if you can afford something,
you probably can't.

∾:∾

Much more pleasant to buy things than
to try to make a living selling them.

∾:∾

Most people have too much credit
for their own wealth.

∾:∾

It is always a good time to invest in kindness.

∾:∾

The Christians must shop fervently at Christmas,
or God will smite the economy.

~:~

How appropriate that a nation of debtors should
be ruled by a government that runs on debt.

~:~

To the poor, interest is something that you pay;
for the wealthy it is something that you collect.

~:~

In a wealthy country the rich are thinner than the
poor; in a very poor country it is the reverse.

~:~

A trip to Las Vegas is a bet against the house.

~:~

If you want to waste your life, believe that making
a lot of money is going to make you happy.

~:~

Never complain about the price of something you
bought—it was worth that price because some
fool was willing to pay it.

∼:∼

The less you want, the less you need;
the more you want, the more you need.

∼:∼

In very backward countries people foolishly believe
that being with family and friends
is more important than money.

∼:∼

The real poor complain very little,
as they expect nothing.

∼:∼

If you are wealthy money is like the air;
if you are poor it is like the moon.

∼:∼

Most wealth has been reduced to numbers on a
monthly statement—it has no other real existence
than in the belief systems of capitalism.

∾:∾

How long will I have to work to pay
for this thing I am about to buy?

∾:∾

If you really know money, it will come to you,
in good times or bad.

∾:∾

Would a dog work like a dog to pay
for a bigger doghouse?

∾:∾

I followed all the rules—so where is the money?

∾:∾

Business is largely an exchange of money
between people who were born to make it
and people who were born to lose it.

∾:∾

Suppose you could be twice as rich but
it took half your life to get there?

~:~

Poverty appreciates everything—
wealth only the best.

~:~

Shopping is like sex, in that desires
are aroused and then satisfied.

~:~

In America we save empty jars, grocery bags,
redwoods, whales, the planet—
everything but money.

~:~

Casinos are organized on the principle that people
wish to lose their money as efficiently as possible.

~:~

Heaven would be filled with big tippers
if God were a waitress.

~:~

People who are competent with their money
worry the most, and people who are
incompetent with it worry the least.

∾:∾

A real man knows how to fix anything,
but a wimp knows how to make a lot of
money to hire people to fix anything.

∾:∾

The hateful thing about insurance
is that something bad has to happen for you
to get any value from it.

∾:∾

The immigrant who fails to learn the language is
money in the bank for his countryman who does.

∾:∾

Money is like water: it seeks its own level;
we are most comfortable with those who have
about the same amount of it as we do.

∾:∾

The rich keep busy because
they fear being seen as idle.

~:~

Cheap money is for sale to the rich
and expensive money is for sale to the poor.

~:~

If we'd known then what we know now,
we would all be millionaires.

~:~

Spending all your money during your lifetime
is like being your own heir.

~:~

Investing is always a gamble,
but gamblers make poor investors.

~:~

People who are born to make money
understand economics better than any economist.

~:~

The only difference between the amateur and the
professional investor is that the amateur
buys at the peak and sells at the bottom.

~:~

The laws of economics are continually
being rewritten by human ingenuity.

~:~

Just think of where we might be now if only we
had blah, blah, blah when blah, blah, blah....

~:~

New money can't bear anything
that is even slightly shabby.

~:~

We never tire of reading of millionaires
who are sent to jail.

~:~

A very easy job makes for a very long day at work.

∼:∼

Luckiest are those who always knew
what they wanted to do in life.

∼:∼

Sometimes you have to do the work
and hope the career materializes.

∼:∼

Some people hit the playground running.

∼:∼

The best way to work with people who
get things done is to stay out of their way.

∼:∼

Difficult people enjoy meetings—
impossible people adore them.

∼:∼

You knew the nail was bending,
so why did you keep hitting it?

~:~

There are a thousand ways to prostitute yourself,
sex being only one of them.

~:~

The boss may complain, but does he offer
to swap jobs with you?

~:~

I'm not lazy — I just like to work gently.

~:~

The first lesson of serving the rich
is to become invisible.

~:~

A simple exchange of time for money —
it's called a job.

~:~

In exchanging time for money most people
discover that their time is worth very little.

~:~

There is as much dignity, and as much
humiliation, in cleaning the toilets in the
White House as there is in being president.

~:~

For most people, the job is the life: a man does not
say that he is a father and a husband,
he says that he is a carpenter.

~:~

If you are a lawyer, for God's sake don't talk like
one with your friends—there are no rules of
evidence in real life.

~:~

No one who serves is ever really grateful
for a gratuity.

~:~

A job is a collar that chafes.

∼:∼

Every job description contains a little humiliation.

∼:∼

There is no job description that contains
the word "security."

∼:∼

I'm not afraid of hard work—being at home
with my family, now that's scary!

∼:∼

To say something is "academic" reveals the
lack of respect we have for those who teach.

∼:∼

Coffee brings the mind to work, and
alcohol enables the mind to leave it.

∼:∼

No one knows more, and is paid less,
than a farmer.

∾:∾

Do what needs to be done,
without talking it to death.

∾:∾

On a planet on which a day is eighty-seven hours
long, I might manage to clear my desk.

∾:∾

Retirement is having three and a half
weekends a week.

∾:∾

The first rule of operating heavy equipment
is to not kill the guy with the shovel.

∾:∾

A lawyer pleads for the freedom of a man
he would hate to meet in a dark alley.

∾:∾

Once you discover that you are actually good at
something, you begin to think that you
might be good at other things.

~:~

A deadline alters time and space—one can
accomplish a month of work in the day before it.

~:~

Compared to a farm or a factory,
an office is a very unproductive place.

~:~

Comfortably wrapped in my white skin, I grumble
about preferences for people of other colors.

~:~

People who pretend to have a career
are actually rather common.

~:~

A pedant has many ways to
amplify a small thought.

~:~

A true perfectionist never finishes anything.

~:~

Jobs have grown wings.

~:~

We take for granted the competence
of the men who maintain elevators,
but not that of presidents and CEOs.

~:~

If you would like to achieve an office
with a view at an early age, become a roofer.

~:~

Networking in a roomful of networkers
is like going fishing in a fish market.

~:~

We Americans are good at driving large trucks,
but we prefer to import our doctors and engineers.

~:~

Don't do any work that you
wouldn't sign your name to.

~:~

The "meeting face" is an alert mask concealing a
mind that is occupied with personal matters.

~:~

There are few secrets of success, but plenty of
people making a good living selling them.

~:~

We do ten things poorly,
when we should be doing one thing well.

~:~

At peak performance there is nothing in the
universe but the task at hand.

~:~

Be interested in everything and
every place will be interesting.

∻

Travel addiction is a form of boredom with life.

∻

It's the other tourists who ruin the good places.

∻

Drive at the speed limit and you will
discover a fascinating road.

∻

Cities only reveal their secret charms to walkers.

∻

The here and now is the most fascinating journey.

∻

TRAVEL

For thousands of years man dreamed of being able
to fly—now we dream of being upgraded
to Business Class so we can stretch our legs.

~:~

The world is an inconvenient, corrupt, dangerous,
dirty, disease-infested place—if you travel.

~:~

Sometimes the high point of a vacation is coming
home and being among your own things again.

~:~

A common misconception is
that spiritual journeys require travel.

~:~

The best travelers never complain—
the worst never stop.

~:~

For comfortable accommodations,
try staying home.

~:~

Sardines in a can travel more comfortably
than one who flies in Coach.

∼:∼

Watching people at the airport is far more
interesting than the book on your lap.

∼:∼

Traveling can be a lot of work,
just to be somewhere else.

∼:∼

Vacations have been robbed of all leisure.

∼:∼

After a long airplane flight I feel as if
someone had erased part of my brain.

∼:∼

A tour group could travel through hell and find it
charming, but the accommodations
and service not worth the price.

∼:∼

I've seen plays that are longer than my life.

∼:∼

I believe in any religion that has celestial music.

∼:∼

Everyone knew music until
recording was invented.

∼:∼

There should be no such thing as a concert hall
without a dance floor.

∼:∼

There is music that makes you dance,
even if you don't.

∼:∼

Fiction is gossip about imaginary friends.

∼:∼

The problem with fiction is that it is just that.

~:~

The most valuable thing in my wallet
is my library card.

~:~

You are always at home in an art museum,
because art is a universal language.

~:~

On matters of taste, everyone is always right.

~:~

Computers increase writing
while decreasing literacy.

~:~

Call me a serious music listener and I will smile.

~:~

There are patterns and rhythms everywhere
if you can see them and hear them.

~:~

The movies get longer and the popcorn gets bigger,
and there is about as much substance
in each of them.

~:~

Art worth consuming ripens
in about a hundred years.

~:~

There is nothing more conducive to falling asleep
than propping myself up in bed with a book
I have been looking forward to reading.

~:~

We must grant young artists the courtesy of
pretending to be outraged by their spirited
attempts, but the truth is that nothing outrages us
anymore.

~:~

A writer must write, and write and write.

~:~

At the symphony half close their eyes
to concentrate on the music
and the other half to sleep.

~:~

Writers should give thanks that a Shakespeare
only comes along once in 400 years.

~:~

To write well you must be a ruthless editor.

~:~

A poem can only be translated
by writing another poem.

~:~

Fiction writing is an attempt
to make a story go somewhere.

~:~

Money follows culture,
because culture validates money.

~:~

There are writers who have
exactly one perfect book in them.

~:~

To be a good writer,
allow very few adverbs into your life.

~:~

Rock is a concert at which it is impossible to sleep.

~:~

Hollywood has sunk to the point where
Oscars are awarded for mumbling.

~:~

A poem should be more like a painting
than like a novel.

~:~

An autobiography is just an authorized biography.

~:~

You will find few murder-mystery readers in the
neighborhoods where people are often murdered.

~:~

Any articulate person is capable of creating an epigram because the raw material of an epigram is having lived while thinking. There is something thrilling about hearing yourself quoted. You have said something worth repeating. You are a sage! It is a little taste of immortality. You begin to dream of a spot in *Bartlett's Familiar Quotations.*

If you would like to try your hand, write out an observation or an opinion. Don't worry about how many words it takes to express the thought. Examine your idea. What is the essence of it? Begin to trim unnecessary clauses and words. Always keep in mind the immortal words of Strunk & White in *The Elements of Style:* "Omit unnecessary words."

If you get stuck, leave it and return later, always looking for the essence of your thought. The original thought may change; a new thought will emerge. You are trying for brevity—but if you have something worth saving, two or three lines are acceptable.

Try not to use long Latin words, adverbs, proper names, slang, topical references, qualifiers, foreign words or expressions, parenthetical statements, suppositions, or ephemeral expressions. Plain language will do. Think big. Don't try to be clever. You are looking for something timeless about the human condition.

Suggestions for Further Reading

The Penguin Dictionary of Epigrams, M. J. Cohen,
Penguin Books, 2001.

The introduction distinguishes epigrams as being shorter and sharper than most short quotations. This huge collection is my favorite anthology of epigrams; but the paperback edition is printed in small type that might be difficult for older eyes.

The Maxims of the Duc de la La Rochefoucauld,
Wingate Publishers, 1957, trans. C. Fitzgibbon.

There are many translations; a good one is by Constantine Fitzgibbon. La Rochefoucauld (1613–1680) remains the gold standard of epigrammists. He led a turbulent life of love, war, and politics, in and out of favor with the French court, losing and regaining fortunes, one of the leading intellects of the seventeenth century.

*"No man is more frequently in error
than he who cannot bear to be wrong."*

Culture and Value, Ludwig Wittgenstein,
University of Chicago Press, 1980, trans. Peter Winch

Wittgenstein taught his philosophy through epigrams, parables, cryptic remarks, and anecdotes. His main subject was the difficulty of communicating through language and he raised problems that almost brought philosophy to a complete stop. He has many terse but brilliant insights on art and religion.

> *"Genius is talent in which character
> makes itself heard."*

Life's Little Instruction Book, H. Jackson Brown, Jr.,
Rutledge Hill Press, 1991.

A very popular book and for good reasons. Originally written as a gift for his son when he started college. Five hundred eleven short pieces of very good advice on how to live a happy and rewarding life. I have read and reread it many times to my benefit. There are a number of sequels, but the original is my favorite.